Read Now
For Beginning ESL Students

Iris Ramer
Middlesex County College

KENDALL/HUNT PUBLISHING COMPANY
4050 Westmark Drive   Dubuque, Iowa 52002

Copyright © 2008 by Iris Ramer

ISBN 978-0-7575-5076-8

Kendall/Hunt Publishing Company has the exclusive rights to reproduce this work,
to prepare derivative works from this work, to publicly distribute this work,
to publicly perform this work and to publicly display this work.

Printed in the United States of America
10 9 8 7 6 5 4 3 2 1

CONTENTS

ACKNOWLEDGMENTS

I would like to express my gratitude to my ESL students for all their support and positive response to my work.

I am grateful to Karen Gormish for her help and her great computer skills in preparing this manuscript.

Finally, I would like to thank my children Michael and Neil for their patience and understanding, and especially my husband, Elliot, for his continual support and encouragement.

PREFACE

TO THE TEACHER:

The purpose of *Read Now* is to provide beginning ESL students at the adult and young adult levels with reading practice using short compositions. It does not simply provide an opportunity for students to read the text, but rather encourages them to become independent readers. There are fifteen units in the book, giving students the opportunity to read while focusing on simple sentences and using the simple present tense. In addition, some of the units introduce the present progressive and simple future tenses. All of the chapters have a short composition written in a descriptive mode, followed by exercises to select the main idea and identify the correct part of speech. Following that is a true-or-false exercise, and then a writing project. At the end of the book, a reading journal has been included so that students can have the opportunity to begin building their own vocabulary list of words. Additional pages are included for vocabulary work such as spelling quizzes. In sum, *Read Now* gives beginning ESL students the opportunity to read, and also provides a number of reading comprehension exercises for continual practice.

TO THE STUDENT:

This book will give you the opportunity to practice reading in English at a beginning level. In addition to the book, you will need some notebook paper, a pen, a pencil, and an English dictionary. Let us begin.

UNIT 1

Reading

I. Please read the following composition:

Reading is one of the most important things we can do. There are two reasons for this.

First, if we are trying to learn English, we have to read as much as possible so that we can learn how to speak better. It is very difficult to learn a language only by hearing people speak. Also, when we practice reading as much as we can, it makes it easier for us to understand American people when they speak. If we have an easier time understanding, we will also have an easier time speaking.

Second, by reading we can learn many things about life in the United States. If we learn to understand American life better, it becomes much easier for us to live in this country. We have more opportunities, and that makes it easier for us to help our families–which is the reason why we are here.

Many people are afraid to read. Some people do not know how to read well in their own language. Others do know how to read, but when they pick up a newspaper or a magazine in English, they do not know where to begin. There are so many articles that they feel like it is too much for them.

A very good strategy is to choose one article–only one–and read that article carefully. This may take a couple of days, or even a week or more. But it does not matter how long it takes. The important thing is that we are getting practice in reading. If we keep on doing that every day, we will improve our English, and our life in this country will become easier.

II. What do you think is the main idea of this passage? Circle your answer.

    A. We are here in order to help our families.

    B. Many people are afraid to read.

    C. Reading makes it easier for us to learn to speak and understand English.

    D. Some people do not read well in their own language.

III. Give the part of speech of each of the following words:

1. we

2. are

3. for

4. is

5. country

6. an

7. in

8. English

9. people

10. newspaper

IV. True or False? Answer "T" for true and "F" for false.

_____ 1. When we pick up a newspaper, there are many articles in it.

_____ 2. When we read the newspaper, we should not take much time in reading the articles.

_____ 3. Everyone likes to read.

_____ 4. Not everyone is good at reading in their own language.

_____ 5. Learning to understand America makes our lives here more complicated.

_____ 6. We came here to help our families.

_____ 7. Reading is not a very important part of our life in this country.

_____ 8. It is not easy to learn a language only by hearing people speak.

_____ 9. Some people cannot decide where to start when they pick up a newspaper or a magazine in English.

_____ 10. If we have an easier time understanding English, that does not mean we will have an easier time speaking it.

V. Write correct English sentences using the following words:

1. it

2. English

3. a

4. we

5. speak

6. reading

7. families

8. are

9. have

10. help

Unit 2

Television

I. Please read the following composition:

Everyone likes to watch television. But sometimes, we think that maybe television is not such a good thing.

There are many channels, and everyone can find a show that they are interested in, even in the middle of the night. Television shows help us to pass the time, and to relax.

Very often, we can watch television shows in our own language. We like that, because we can understand what is going on, and also because it reminds us of home. But it can also be a problem, because we do not learn English that way. Watching television in English is much more difficult than watching in our own language. But if we watch English-language TV every day, after awhile it will help us to understand English better. If we understand the language more easily, it will help us to speak better. But this takes time; it does not happen in one week or one month.

Television can be a good thing for children, too, but it can also be a very bad thing for them. If they neglect their school work because they are watching too much television, that is a very serious problem. Also, there are many things on television that children should not see. We try to prevent them from watching channels that are not good for them, and from watching at times that are not good for them. But we cannot always do that.

So, television can be both good and bad. We do the best we can to use it in ways that are good. As for the things about it that are bad, we do the best we can to keep them under control.

II. What do you think is the main idea of this passage? Circle your
answer.

   A. We can improve our English by watching television, but it takes
       time.

   B. There are things on television that are not good for children.

   C. Television is both good and bad.

   D. We can watch television shows in our own language.

III. Give the part of speech of each of the following words:

   1. the

   2. can

   3. sometimes

   4. but

   5. in

   6. and

   7. likes

   8. they

   9. children

   10. always

IV. True or False? Answer with "T" for true and "F" for false.

_____ 1. A problem with television is that there are not enough channels.

_____ 2. There are television shows at all hours of the day and night.

_____ 3. There are often television shows in our own language.

_____ 4. Watching shows in our own language helps us to improve our English.

_____ 5. Watching shows in our own language is easier than watching shows in English.

_____ 6. If we watch shows in English, this will help us to improve our English very quickly.

_____ 7. We do not have to worry about what children see on television.

_____ 8. We have to worry about children neglecting their homework in order to watch television shows.

_____ 9. We do not allow children to watch channels that are not good for them.

_____ 10. We try to prevent children from watching television at the wrong times.

V. Write correct English sentences using the following words:

1. television

2. it

3. sometimes

4. one

5. watch

6. they

7. but

8. there

9. are

10. every day

UNIT 3

A Visit to Brooklyn

I. Please read the following composition:

When people think about visiting New York City, what they usually have in mind is Manhattan. But another very interesting place to visit is Brooklyn.

You can drive to Brooklyn, but traffic and parking can be a problem. Or, you can take the train to Manhattan and then change to a subway train for Brooklyn. If you do that, you can choose different subway lines that will take you to different parts of Brooklyn.

Here is one suggestion: Take the A train in the downtown direction to the High Street stop. You must hope that the escalator is running; otherwise, you will have to walk up a very long flight of stairs to the street. But when you get there, you will find the path that leads out onto the Brooklyn Bridge. Many people like to walk across the Brooklyn Bridge, to admire the architecture and to see spectacular views. It is one of the most important landmarks of New York.

People who like to look at beautiful buildings should visit the famous Park Slope neighborhood. Take the downtown F train to the Seventh Avenue stop. As you walk through the streets, you will see block after block filled with beautiful houses. Unfortunately, they are very, very expensive.

These are only two of the many interesting things that you will find if you visit Brooklyn. People who want to understand New York City should spend time in Brooklyn. There are many important things that you can learn there.

II. What do you think is the main idea of this passage? Circle your answer.

    A. There are different subway lines that lead to different parts of Brooklyn.

    B. The Brooklyn Bridge is one of New York's most important landmarks.

    C. You can go to Brooklyn by car or by train.

    D. Even though Manhattan is what most people think about when they think of New York, Brooklyn is also a very interesting part of the city.

III. Give the part of speech of each of the following words:

1. usually

2. Brooklyn

3. visit

4. you

5. walk

6. must

7. the

8. things

9. to

10. in

IV. True or False? Answer with "T" for true and "F" for false.

_____ 1. It is easy to drive to Brooklyn.

_____ 2. If you take the train to Manhattan, you have to change to a subway train to get to Brooklyn.

_____ 3. At the High Street subway stop, the subway station is very close to the street level.

_____ 4. Walking across the Brooklyn Bridge is a very popular activity.

_____ 5. The Brooklyn Bridge is an important structure for people who are interested in architecture.

_____ 6. The problem with the Brooklyn Bridge is that when you are on it, you cannot see anything important.

_____ 7. The Seventh Avenue stop on the F train is located in the Park Slope neighborhood.

_____ 8. Park Slope is primarily an area of factories and warehouses.

_____ 9. It is easy to buy a house in the Park Slope neighborhood.

_____ 10. For people who want to understand New York City, it is important to visit Brooklyn.

V. Write correct English sentences using the following words:

1. usually

2. street

3. it

4. beautiful

5. visit

6. Manhattan

7. you

8. the

9. people

10. drive

UNIT 4

School

I. Please read the following composition:

Going to school is extremely important for us. That is why we come to school even though we have to work long hours, and also take care of our families. We usually set up our schedules so that we can take classes in the morning. That way, we can go to our jobs in the afternoon and at night.

For us, the most important class is ESL. Why? Because we have to improve our English before we can do anything else. Some of us have hopes of studying for a profession here in America, but we cannot do that unless we improve our English. Also, we have to become better at English if we want to advance in our jobs. Finally, if we want to help our children with their homework, we have to know English well.

In our ESL classes, we meet people from every part of the world. There are students from many different Hispanic countries, and also from Middle Eastern countries like Egypt, Lebanon, and Iran. We sometimes meet people from Russia, Poland, and the Ukraine. Also, there are students from China, Korea, and Vietnam. And we often meet people from India and Pakistan. Sometimes, people from those countries already know some English, but they just need some extra practice.

When we meet people from all these different countries, it makes our world bigger. It makes our lives more interesting. We have experiences in our ESL classes that we cannot have anywhere else.

II. What do you think is the main idea of this passage? Circle your answer.

    A. Some of us have hopes of studying for a profession in America.

    B. Going to school is very important for us, because it helps us to improve our English and it makes our lives more interesting.

    C. We usually set up our schedules so that we can take classes in the morning.

    D. We want to help our children with their homework.

III. Give the part of speech of each of the following words:

1. we

2. usually

3. in

4. classes

5. often

6. meet

7. from

8. Korea

9. cannot

10. go

IV. True or False? Answer with "T" for true and "F" for false.

_____ 1. In spite of working long hours, nevertheless we come to school.

_____ 2. We study in the morning, and we work in the afternoon and at night.

_____ 3. Computer classes are the most important classes that we take.

_____ 4. In order to be able to study for a profession in America, we have to improve our English.

_____ 5. Even if we do not know English well, we can still help our children with their homework.

_____ 6. Our ESL class is important because we have to improve our English in order to do the things we want to do.

_____ 7. The problem with our ESL class is that we only meet people from our own countries.

_____ 8. In our ESL class, we seldom meet people from India or Pakistan.

_____ 9. It is not unusual for us to meet people from Korea and Vietnam.

_____ 10. Because of our ESL class, our world is very small and our lives are boring.

V. Write correct English sentences using the following words:

1. students

2. in the morning

3. important

4. homework

5. meet

6. know

7. seldom

8. come

9. go

10. it

UNIT 5

Staying in Good Health

I. Please read the following composition:

We try to do the best we can to stay healthy. We hope to stay in good health by eating the right foods, getting enough rest, and exercising regularly.

But, in fact, it is very hard to do these things. Very often, we have so many responsibilities that it is hard for us to get enough rest, and we do not have time to eat the right foods. Also, when we get home from work and school and finish taking care of our children, we are too tired to exercise.

The really important part of staying healthy is to avoid stress as much as we can. Of course, there is always going to be stress in our lives. We can never avoid that completely. But the idea is to avoid it as much as possible. If we can keep stress to a minimum in our lives, we have a better chance of staying healthy.

An important way to avoid stress is to stay away from news shows and talk shows on television. Those shows make people worry about many things that there really is not much need to worry about. For people who like to watch television, it is better to watch other kinds of shows, such as documentaries, music events, or sports shows. For people who want to know what is happening in the world, it is much better to read the newspaper than to watch the news on television.

We are going to have stress in our lives no matter what we do. But if we avoid stress as much as possible, we have a much better chance of staying healthy.

II. What do you think is the main idea of this passage? Circle your answer.

    A. Taking care of our children absorbs a lot of our energy.

    B. We try to eat the right foods, but we cannot always do that.

    C. We try to do the things that help us to stay healthy, but it is not easy.

    D. We have many responsibilities in our daily lives.

III. Give the part of speech of each of the following words:

    1. people

    2. often

    3. try

    4. shows

    5. it

    6. read

    7. finish

    8. home

    9. is

    10. our

IV. True or false? Answer with "T" for true and "F" for false.

_____ 1. We cannot always exercise.

_____ 2. We can avoid stress if we want to.

_____ 3. We want to avoid all the stress that we can.

_____ 4. If we avoid stress, we will stay healthy.

_____ 5. We should stay away from news shows and talk shows on television, because we cannot understand them.

_____ 6. The problem with television news shows and talk shows is that they increase stress.

_____ 7. People who like to watch television should stay away from sports shows.

_____ 8. Documentaries are good shows to watch for people who want to avoid stress.

_____ 9. There is always going to be some stress in our lives.

_____ 10. Stress does not have any effect on whether we stay healthy or not.

V. Write correct English sentences using the following words:

1. watch

2. often

3. of

4. on

5. worry

6. eat

7. exercise

8. we

9. to

10. good

UNIT 6

Money

I. Please read the following composition:

We need money because we have to pay our bills. But we also have to save money, so we can buy a house, and help our children, and also help our families back home.

There is also another reason why we have to save money. We all know that in the United States we have to work very hard. But that is not enough. We also have to make our money work for us.

How can we do that? The answer: By saving money and then investing it. Many people think we can only do that if we are wealthy. But that is a mistake. If we can save three thousand dollars, we can open an investment account.

There are different kinds of investment accounts. For us, the easiest type to use is called a "mutual fund" (in India and Pakistan, these are called "investment trusts"). For most mutual funds, you can open an account with three thousand dollars. Then, after you have your account, you put more money into it as often as you can. Over time, your money will grow. But you must be patient, because it takes time.

When we open a mutual fund account, there are two basic problems that we have to deal with. First, there are many different types of mutual funds. It can be difficult to decide which is the best type for you. In order to do that, you have to learn about the different kinds of mutual funds, so that you can make a good decision.

Second, various forms of legal documentation are required, such as social security numbers, in order to open an account. So, we have to be sure that we have the documentation we need.

In America, it is important to make our money work for us. We can do that, but we have to learn how to do it.

II. What do you think is the main idea of this passage? Circle your answer.

   A. It is very important for us to save money and learn how to invest it.

   B. In the United States, it is not enough just to work hard.

   C. We do not have to be wealthy to open a mutual fund account.

   D. There are problems involved in opening a mutual fund account.

III. Give the part of speech of each of the following words:

   1. pay

   2. bills

   3. money

   4. takes

   5. problem

   6. know

   7. save

   8. for

   9. you

   10. in

IV. True or False? Answer with "T" for true and "F" for false.

_____ 1. In the United States, we have to make our money work for us.

_____ 2. If we save money and invest it, we can make that money work for us.

_____ 3. Only wealthy people can open investment accounts.

_____ 4. A mutual fund is one type of investment account.

_____ 5. For us, mutual funds are not as easy to use as other types of investment accounts.

_____ 6. For most mutual funds, three thousand dollars is not enough to open an investment account.

_____ 7. When you open a mutual fund account, you must be patient.

_____ 8. You can open a mutual fund account whether or not you have a legal social security number.

_____ 9. There are different types of mutual funds.

_____ 10. There is no need for you to learn about the different types of mutual funds.

V. Write correct English sentences using the following words:

1. money

2. you

3. learn

4. work

5. open

6. with

7. make

8. it

9. help

10. save

UNIT 7

Gardening

I. Please read the following composition:

Gardening is a very popular activity everywhere in the world. Many people garden in order to grow extra food. Others do it just because they like plants and flowers. Some people grow vegetables because they want the vegetables to be fresh, instead of buying them in the supermarket. In warm climates, people do the same thing with fruits.

Some people garden because it helps them to relax. A famous person who does this is Pedro Martinez, the baseball player. He says that gardening helps him to concentrate when he is pitching in baseball games.

Gardening can be hard work. An example of this is the situation where we have to dig up a lawn in order to plant new grass seed. We can rent a machine called a "rototiller" that will help us to do that job. But some people do not feel comfortable using these machines. Also, if the lawn is not extremely large, some people do not want to spend money to rent a rototiller, transport it to their house, and fill it with gasoline. People who are in that situation have to do the work themselves, using a shovel to turn over the earth. It is not easy. We have to be in good health and good physical shape to do that kind of work.

Even when the work is not so hard, being out in the sun for a long time can make people tired. So, gardening is not an easy hobby. But for people who enjoy it, it makes them feel good in their bodies and also in their minds.

II. What do you think is the main idea of this passage? Circle your answer.

A. Some people garden because they like plants and flowers.

B. Gardening is not an easy hobby.

C. Gardening is something that people all over the world like to do, for different reasons.

D. Some people garden because it helps them to relax.

III. Give the part of speech of each of the following words:

1. grow

2. vegetables

3. it

4. helps

5. Pedro Martinez

6. him

7. they

8. want

9. spend

10. to

IV. True or False? Answer with "T" for true and "F" for false.

_____ 1. Many people garden because they want to grow extra food.

_____ 2. Gardening is a good hobby for people who do not want to work hard.

_____ 3. If people want to dig up a lawn in order to plant new grass seed, they have to use a rototiller.

_____ 4. Not everybody likes to use a rototiller.

_____ 5. If we use a rototiller, we need an electric wire so it can run.

_____ 6. If we do not want to use a rototiller, then we have to use a shovel instead.

_____ 7. If a person has been sick recently, it is a good idea for them to use a shovel if they have to dig up their lawn.

_____ 8. People like gardening because it is an easy hobby.

_____ 9. After we have been out in the sun a long time, we may have to rest for a while.

_____ 10. People who enjoy gardening do it even though it makes them have more stress.

V. Write correct English sentences using the following:

1. flowers

2. their

3. new

4. with

5. relax

6. feel

7. easy

8. hobby

9. enjoy

10. makes

UNIT 8

Taxes

I. Please read the following composition:

The tax system in America is one of the biggest problems the country has. It is a problem for two reasons. First, many people believe that the system is unfair. Second, almost everyone agrees that it is too complicated.

People who believe the tax system is unfair argue that there are too many different rates. In their opinion, everybody should pay the same rate. But not everyone agrees with this. Some people think that people who make more money should pay a higher rate.

There is one thing that almost everyone agrees on: The tax system is so complicated that no one really understands it. The United States tax law is thousands of pages long–yes, thousands of pages! Accountants understand it better than most people do, but they do not really understand it either. Accountants often specialize in different aspects of the tax law. But there is probably no one, not even the President of the United States, who completely understands every aspect of the law.

What can be done about this? Some people want to get rid of the whole tax law and start all over again. Others just want to make changes, but without changing the basic law. So far, Americans are not able to agree on what should be done about the tax system. The only thing everyone is able to agree on is that something needs to be done.

II. What do you think is the main idea of this passage? Circle your answer.

    A. Some people want to have an entirely new tax law.

    B. Some people pay higher tax rates than others.

    C. The tax system is one of America's biggest problems.

    D. No one really understands the tax system.

III. Give the part of speech of each of the following words:

    1. should

    2. pages

    3. pay

    4. make

    5. but

    6. the

    7. it

    8. needs

    9. think

    10. believe

IV. True or False? Answer with "T" for true and "F" for false.

_____ 1. Most Americans generally agree that everybody should pay the same tax rate.

_____ 2. Americans generally agree that no one really understands the tax system.

_____ 3. Americans generally agree that the problem with the tax system is that it is too simple.

_____ 4. The United States tax law is the size of a very large book.

_____ 5. Accountants completely understand the tax law, but no one else completely understands it.

_____ 6. There are accountants who are specialists in different aspects of the tax law.

_____ 7. The President of the United States completely understands the tax law, but no one else completely understands it.

_____ 8. Americans generally agree that the tax law should be completely rewritten.

_____ 9. Americans generally agree that something should be done about the tax system.

_____ 10. Americans do not generally agree about how the tax system should be changed.

V. Write correct English sentences using the following:

1. do not

2. make

3. different

4. but

5. agrees

6. one

7. understand

8. there

9. is

10. pay

UNIT 9

Baseball

I. Please read the following composition:

Baseball is the national game of the United States. It is also the national game of several Hispanic countries, and also of Japan. Today, in the United States, there are top-level players from all over the world: Australia, China, Japan, Korea, Puerto Rico, Cuba, the Dominican Republic, Venezuela, Colombia, Panama, Nicaragua, Mexico, the Netherlands, and of course, Canada and the United States. Many people believe that soon, there are going to be players from Africa.

The baseball season begins in April and continues through the summer. The regular season ends in September. Then, in October, the championship season begins, with the best teams playing against each other. By the end of October, there is a new champion team, and the season is over.

Every four years, the World Baseball Classic is played. The World Baseball Classic is similar to the Soccer World Cup, except for one thing: Any country that wants to send a team can do so. At the moment, the World Baseball Classic champion is Japan.

Baseball is a symbol of America. Every baseball team has players from many different countries–just like America. And if you go to watch a baseball game you will find spectators from many different countries. They speak many different languages, eat different types of food, have different cultures, but they all belong to the Nation of Baseball. Another word for "the Nation of Baseball" is: America.

II. What do you think is the main idea of this passage? Circle your
answer.

A. Any country can send a team to the World Baseball Classic.

B. Baseball is like America: People coming together from many
different countries of the world.

C. Baseball is the national game of a number of countries, including
the United States.

D. In the United States, baseball is played during the summer months.

III. Give the part of speech of each of the following words:

1. baseball

2. at

3. Puerto Rico

4. from

5. years

6. begins

7. players

8. find

9. ends

10. new

IV. True or false? Answer "T" for true and "F" for false.

_____ 1. Today in the United States, there are top-level baseball players from several Hispanic countries.

_____ 2. There are no top-level Asian players.

_____ 3. In the near future, there may be top-level players from Africa.

_____ 4. The baseball season in the United States begins in the month of April and continues until the end of August.

_____ 5. In September, the championship season begins.

_____ 6. The season comes to an end in the month of October.

_____ 7. People who are not from the United States generally do not go to baseball games.

_____ 8. Most American people regard baseball as an important part of American life.

_____ 9. The World Baseball Classic is a special event that takes place every year.

_____ 10. The Nation of Baseball is another way of saying "America."

V. Write correct English sentences using the following words:

1. September

2. team

3. watch

4. game

5. wants

6. has

7. find

8. begins

9. speak

10. countries

UNIT 10

Christmas in New York

I. Please read the following composition:

Christmas is a very special time. It is full of excitement. Children wonder what their gifts are going to be. So many people go to the stores that the parking lots are completely filled with cars.

In New York City, in Rockefeller Center, there is an enormous Christmas tree. It is hung with thousands of lights. People come from all over America, and from all over the world, to see it. Every evening during the month of December, there are thousands of people in Rockefeller Center and the streets around it, looking at the beautiful decorations.

Across the street from Rockefeller Center, Saks Fifth Avenue has beautiful displays in its store windows. On both sides of Fifth Avenue, from Rockefeller Center up to 59th Street, every building has special Christmas displays, especially the famous stores like Tiffany's, Bergdorf Goodman, and Cartier.

When we join the crowds in front of the Rockefeller Center Christmas tree, we feel like we are part of something bigger than ourselves. For those few moments, we forget that we are not originally from America. We forget that we are still learning English. We become completely part of the United States. We become American.

This year, if you can, go to Rockefeller Center in the month of December. Become a part of that special feeling. But do not go there by car, because the traffic is tremendous. And if you go with your children, keep them very close to you, so that all of you can enjoy a special evening together.

II. What is the main idea of this passage? Circle your answer.

    A. When we visit Rockefeller Center at Christmas time, we feel like we are part of America.

    B. When we visit Rockefeller Center at Christmas time, we can see the famous Christmas tree hung with thousands of lights.

    C. When we visit Rockefeller Center at Christmas time, we see beautiful displays in the surrounding stores.

    D. When we visit Rockefeller Center at Christmas time, we must keep our children very close to us.

III. Give the part of speech of each of the following words:

1. gifts

2. go

3. world

4. lights

5. New York

6. it

7. forget

8. an

9. up

10. see

IV. True or False? Answer with "T" for true and "F" for false.

_____ 1. People avoid going to stores during the Christmas season.

_____ 2. During the Christmas season, only American people go to Rockefeller Center.

_____ 3. People who go to Rockefeller Center have to keep their children very close to them.

_____ 4. For people who drive to Rockefeller Center during the Christmas season, traffic is not a problem.

_____ 5. There are many famous stores on Fifth Avenue near Rockefeller Center.

_____ 6. During the Christmas season, children think about what gifts they are going to get.

_____ 7. During the Christmas season, it is not easy to find a parking space at stores.

_____ 8. When we go to Rockefeller Center at Christmas time, we do not feel like we have come to the United States from foreign lands.

_____ 9. If you walk up Fifth Avenue from Rockefeller Center to 59th Street during the month of December, you will not notice that it is the Christmas season.

_____ 10. People do not pay much attention to the Christmas tree in Rockefeller Center.

V. Write correct English sentences using the following words:

1. New York City

2. stores

3. December

4. at

5. building

6. are

7. on

8. is

9. go

10. see

UNIT 11

American Football

I. Please read the following composition:

When the summer ends and the autumn begins, people come home from vacation and children go back to school. The leaves on the trees turn beautiful colors. And the football season begins.

Almost all American high schools have football teams. Not all universities have them, but many do. On the high school level, most games are played on Friday night. On the university level, Saturday afternoon is the main time for football games.

It is very exciting to attend an American football game. Large crowds come to cheer their teams. The cheerleaders inspire the spectators to get involved and make a lot of noise whenever their team does something good. The football game is a time for friends to get together. It is one of the most important social events of the school year. That is why even people who do not really understand American football still like to go to the games.

Many people who come from other countries have a hard time understanding American football. But the basic idea is very simple: The team with the ball has four chances to advance ten yards. If they succeed, they get another four chances to advance another ten yards, and so on. If they fail, the other team gets the ball, and the whole process starts again. The idea is to get the ball into the "end zone."

When we have children in high school, it can be a very good thing to go to some of their school's football games. By doing that, we can have a deeper relationship with our children, and we can also learn more about American life.

II. What do you think is the main idea of this passage? Circle your answer.

    A. It is very exciting to attend an American football game.

    B. At an American football game, the spectators become very excited when their team does something good.

    C. If we take an interest in American football, we can learn something about American life and also have a closer relationship with our children.

    D. Many American universities have football teams, though not all do.

III. Give the part of speech of each of the following words:

    1. the

    2. begins

    3. high schools

    4. come

    5. have

    6. on

    7. and

    8. football

    9. people

    10. can

IV. True or False? Answer with "T" for true and "F" for false.

_____ 1. Football teams are not common at American high schools.

_____ 2. All universities in the United States have football teams.

_____ 3. The summer is the season for football.

_____ 4. Most football games on the university level are played on Friday night.

_____ 5. Football games are major social events at schools.

_____ 6. Most people all over the world understand American football.

_____ 7. If a team does not advance at least ten yards in four tries, they lose the ball.

_____ 8. Football teams want to get the ball into the "end zone."

_____ 9. When we have children in high school, it is advisable to go to some of their school's football games.

_____ 10. At a football game, the cheerleaders encourage the spectators to support their team.

V. Write correct English sentences using the following words:

1. begins

2. something

3. friends

4. important

5. go

6. to

7. ball

8. trees

9. Saturday

10. come

UNIT 12

Children

I. Please read the following composition:

When children are small, it is a problem because we have to watch them all the time. They do not understand that some things are dangerous, and we have to be sure that they do not do things that will put them in danger.

Also, we have to make sure that they get proper education. We have to teach them good manners. Then, when they are old enough to go to school, we have to make sure they are learning what they are supposed to learn, that they do their homework every day, and that they obey the rules.

As children grow up, they become more independent. They can do more and more things on their own, without us helping them. We like that, but we are also afraid of it. We know that they can make wrong decisions that will be very bad for them, and we worry about that.

Eventually, children become adults. At that point, we can no longer control them. We can only hope that we have raised them properly and taught them the right values. But we worry about many things. We worry about our children being with friends who may lead them in wrong directions. We worry about whether the children understand that they have to work and earn a living. At the point when boys and girls form couples, we worry about whether they will be happy together.

At every age, from the time they are born until they grow up to be adults, we worry about our children. But in spite of that, we still want to have children. That never changes.

II. What do you think is the main idea of this passage? Circle your answer.

A. We have to teach our children good manners.

B. Whether they are small or big, children present us with many problems. But in spite of that, we still want to have children.

C. We have to teach children to do their homework every day, and to obey rules.

D. When children are adults, we can no longer control them.

III. Give the part of speech of each of the following words:

1. children

2. small

3. get

4. worry

5. do

6. homework

7. on

8. their

9. become

10. adults

IV. True or False? Answer with "T" for true and "F" for false.

_____ 1. When children are small, they know which things are dangerous and which are not.

_____ 2. It is our responsibility to make sure that children get proper education.

_____ 3. When children go to school, we have to teach them that homework is something that has to be done every day.

_____ 4. As children grow up, we can be sure that they will make the right decisions.

_____ 5. As children grow up, we have mixed feelings about the fact that they can do more and more things on their own.

_____ 6. Even though we know that children can make wrong decisions, we do not worry about that.

_____ 7. When children become adults, we are confident that they understand that they have to work and earn a living.

_____ 8. When children become adults, we are concerned that their friends may convince them to do wrong things.

_____ 9. We know that when boys and girls form couples, they will be happy.

_____ 10. Parents will always worry about their children.

V. Write correct English sentences using the following words:

1. children

2. teach

3. bad

4. may

5. to

6. have

7. it

8. them

9. at

10. worry

UNIT 13

Cars

I. Please read the following composition:

In most places in the United States, people need to have cars in order to get from one place to another. This can cause many problems. When we have a car, we feel like we have a special freedom, because we can drive to any place where there is a road, any time we want to. But that freedom comes with a very high price, because having a car is a big responsibility.

Buying a car is very expensive. But buying the car is only the beginning. We have to register the car. We have to keep it in good condition. We have to have insurance. And, of course, we have to keep it filled with gasoline. These things cost money, and the fact that we have to spend so much money on cars means that we have less money for other things that may be just as important.

On top of that, in order to register our car we have to have a driver's license. That can be a very big problem, because in many states, we have to be able to prove that we are legal residents of the United States in order to apply for a license. If we cannot prove that, we are in a difficult situation.

If we drive a car that is not registered, the police will arrest us almost immediately. Even if the car is registered, if we are driving it without a license and we are stopped by the police, we will be in serious trouble.

There are some places in the United States where people do not need cars. In New York City, for example, there are hundreds of thousands of people who do not have cars. If you know how to take subway trains and busses, you can travel anywhere in the city and even far beyond the city limits. But most places are not like New York.

We like the benefits of having a car, but we do not like the responsibilities. Unfortunately, we cannot have one without the other. If we want to have a car, we have to accept the bad along with the good.

II. What do you think is the main idea of this passage? Circle your answer.

   A. There are many good things about having a car, but there are also many bad things about it.

   B. Having a car is expensive.

   C. Getting a driver's license can be a problem.

   D. Not everyone needs a car.

III. Give the part of speech of each of the following words:

   1. in

   2. car

   3. us

   4. police

   5. is

   6. a

   7. gasoline

   8. we

   9. need

   10. have

IV. True or False? Answer "T" for true and "F" for false.

_____ 1. Most Americans do not need cars.

_____ 2. With a car, we can travel where we want to travel if there is a
            road there.

_____ 3. There are many expenses involved in having a car.

_____ 4. Registration of cars is optional in the United States.

_____ 5. When we have a car, insurance is obligatory in the United
            States.

_____ 6. Driving an unregistered car is not a problem.

_____ 7. We can buy a car and register it, and then get a driver's license
            so we can drive it.

_____ 8. A car is not a necessity in New York City.

_____ 9. In most places, like in New York City, a car is not necessary.

_____ 10. We cannot have a car without the problems that go with it.

V. Write correct English sentences using the following words:

1. cars

2. big

3. there

4. are

5. important

6. because

7. drive

8. New York City

9. can

10. money

UNIT 14

Stress

I. Please read the following composition:

Why do people have so much stress in their lives in the United States?

That is a difficult question to answer. We know that we feel more stress in the United States than we do in our home countries. But we do not have the time to think about why we feel that way. We are too busy working, going to school, and taking care of our families.

Maybe that is answer to the question: We do not have enough time. But why not? Maybe it is because we have more responsibilities here than in our home countries, and we do not have as much help. In our countries, there is always someone to watch the children, but here we have to do it ourselves or pay for someone to do it. In the United States we have more things than in our countries–but we have to work harder to pay for them. Also, in the United States we have hopes of moving up in American society. That is a very powerful dream for us. But to turn the dream into reality, we have to work very hard. Even then, we do not know whether we will accomplish the dream in our lifetime. So we have a lot of uncertainty in our lives.

On top of that, we have to live every day in a strange country, where we do not understand the customs and we have a problem with the language. That is exhausting. So we look forward to going home on vacation. We feel like we will finally be able to relax for awhile. But we cannot, because life back home has become too slow for us. We cannot wait to get back to the United States, where we can relax. Back home, there is too much stress.

II. What do you think is the main idea of this passage? Circle your answer.

    A. When we go home on vacation, we cannot relax.

    B. In the United States, we have more possessions than in our countries.

    C. In our home countries, there is always someone to watch the children, but in the United States we have to do it ourselves or pay someone to do it.

    D. The problem of stress, and why we have it, is very difficult to explain.

III. Give the part of speech of each of the following words:

    1. vacation

    2. we

    3. feel

    4. a

    5. do

    6. have

    7. watch

    8. the

    9. is

    10. always

IV. True or False? Answer with "T" for true and "F" for false.

_____ 1. We are too busy to think about why we feel stress in the United States.

_____ 2. We have more responsibilities and less help in the United States than in our countries.

_____ 3. It is easy for us to have more things in the United States than in our home countries.

_____ 4. We accept that, because we are new in this country, we cannot move up in American society.

_____ 5. We know that we are going to accomplish the dream of moving up in American society.

_____ 6. The dream of moving up in American society requires a lot of hard work.

_____ 7. We can relax when we go back to our countries on vacation.

_____ 8. When we have to live our daily lives in a situation where we have trouble with the language, that makes us very tired.

_____ 9. Compared to the United States, life in our home countries is very fast.

_____ 10. When we go back to our countries on vacation, we find a lot of stress there.

V. Write correct English sentences using the following words:

1. we

2. have

3. home

4. stress

5. our

6. pay

7. work

8. live

9. language

10. know

UNIT 15

Immigration

I. Please read the following composition:

      Immigration is one of the biggest problems in the United States today. Americans are not able to agree on what the country's immigration policy should be.

      Some people want to stop immigration completely, but few people agree with this. According to public opinion polls, most Americans want immigration to continue. There are two main reasons for this. First, most Americans are themselves descendants of immigrants, and they think other people should get the same opportunity. Second, most Americans know that immigrants are hard workers, and that they do jobs no one else wants to do.

      According to polls, most Americans want immigration to continue, but they want it to be controlled. They do not want people to come into the United States secretly, without any legal authorization. But unless the system changes, many people can only get in that way.

      The problem is to decide how the system should be changed. That is where Americans do not agree. There are many different ideas for changing the immigration system, but all of them have some sort of problem, and none of them has wide public support.

      Americans must recognize that no immigration system can ever be perfect. Also, they must accept that no system can be permanent. There will always be a need for changes of one kind or another.

II. What do you think is the main idea of this passage? Circle your answer.

A. Most Americans want immigration to continue.

B. Some Americans want immigration to be stopped.

C. Americans have a problem agreeing on what immigration policy they want.

D. Most Americans want immigration to be controlled.

III. Give the part of speech of each of the following words:

1. want

2. get

3. in

4. decide

5. should

6. for

7. Americans

8. tho

9. workers

10. to

IV. True or False? Answer with "T" for true and "F" for false.

_____ 1. Immigration is a major issue in the United States.

_____ 2. Most people agree that immigration should be stopped.

_____ 3. The Federal Bureau of Investigation (the "FBI") has discovered that most Americans want immigration to continue.

_____ 4. The ancestors of most Americans came to the United States as immigrants.

_____ 5. Most Americans complain that immigrants do not work hard enough.

_____ 6. Most Americans think that immigrants do the jobs other people do not want to do.

_____ 7. Most Americans think that immigration should be controlled.

_____ 8. It does not bother most Americans if people come into the United States without legal authorization.

_____ 9. Most Americans agree on how the immigration system should be changed.

_____ 10. Americans cannot expect to find a perfect immigration system.

V. Write correct English sentences using the following words:

1. know

2. wants

3. to

4. they

5. two

6. where

7. system

8. the

9. agree

10. them

Reading Journal

Name: _____   Date: _____

_____

_____

_____

_____

_____

_____

_____

_____

_____

_____

_____

_____

_____

_____

_____

_____

_____

_____

Name: _____   Date: _____

_____

_____

_____

_____

_____

_____

_____

_____

_____

_____

_____

_____

_____

_____

_____

_____

_____

Name: _____   Date: _____

_____

_____

_____

_____

_____

_____

_____

_____

_____

_____

_____

_____

_____

_____

_____

_____

_____

_____

Name: _____   Date: _____

_____

_____

_____

_____

_____

_____

_____

_____

_____

_____

_____

_____

_____

_____

_____

_____

_____

Name: _____   Date: _____

_____

_____

_____

_____

_____

_____

_____

_____

_____

_____

_____

_____

_____

_____

_____

_____

_____

Name: _____   Date: _____

_____

_____

_____

_____

_____

_____

_____

_____

_____

_____

_____

_____

_____

_____

_____

_____

_____

Name: _____   Date: _____

_____

_____

_____

_____

_____

_____

_____

_____

_____

_____

_____

_____

_____

_____

_____

_____

_____

_____

Name: _____   Date: _____

_____

_____

_____

_____

_____

_____

_____

_____

_____

_____

_____

_____

_____

_____

_____

_____

_____

Name: _____   Date: _____

_____

_____

_____

_____

_____

_____

_____

_____

_____

_____

_____

_____

_____

_____

_____

_____

_____

Name: _____   Date: _____

_____ _____

_____

_____

_____

_____

_____

_____

_____

_____

_____

_____

_____

_____

_____

_____

_____

Name: _____   Date: _____

_____

_____

_____

_____

_____

_____

_____

_____

_____

_____

_____

_____

_____

_____

_____

_____

_____

_____

_____

_____

_____

_____

_____

_____

_____

_____

_____

_____

_____

_____

_____

_____

_____

Name: _____   Date: _____

_____

_____

_____

_____

_____

_____

_____

_____

_____

_____

_____

_____

_____

_____

_____

_____

_____

_____

Name: _____   Date: _____

_____

_____

_____

_____

_____

_____

_____

_____

_____

_____

_____

_____

_____

_____

_____

_____

Name: _____ Date: _____

_____

_____

_____

_____

_____

_____

_____

_____

_____

_____

_____

_____

_____

_____

_____

_____

_____

Name: _____   Date: _____

_____

_____

_____

_____

_____

_____

_____

_____

_____

_____

_____

_____

_____

_____

_____

_____

_____

Name: _____   Date: _____

_____

_____

_____

_____

_____

_____

_____

_____

_____

_____

_____

_____

_____

_____

_____

_____

_____

Name: _____   Date: _____

_____

_____

_____

_____

_____

_____

_____

_____

_____

_____

_____

_____

_____

_____

_____

_____

Name: _____   Date: _____

_____

_____

_____

_____

_____

_____

_____

_____

_____

_____

_____

_____

_____

_____

_____

_____

_____

_____

_____

_____

_____

_____

_____

_____

_____

_____

_____

_____

_____

_____

_____

_____

_____

_____

_____

Vocabulary Work Pages

Name: _____   Date: _____

_____

_____

_____

_____

_____

_____

_____

_____

_____

_____

_____

_____

_____

_____

_____

_____

_____

Name: _____   Date: _____

_____

_____

_____

_____

_____

_____

_____

_____

_____

_____

_____

_____

_____

_____

_____

_____

Name: _____   Date: _____

_____

_____

_____

_____

_____

_____

_____

_____

_____

_____

_____

_____

_____

_____

_____

_____

_____

Name: _____   Date: _____

_____

_____

_____

_____

_____

_____

_____

_____

_____

_____

_____

_____

_____

_____

_____

_____

_____

Name: _____   Date: _____

_____

_____

_____

_____

_____

_____

_____

_____

_____

_____

_____

_____

_____

_____

_____

_____

_____

Name: _____   Date: _____

_____

_____

_____

_____

_____

_____

_____

_____

_____

_____

_____

_____

_____

_____

_____

Name: _____   Date: _____

_____

_____

_____

_____

_____

_____

_____

_____

_____

_____

_____

_____

_____

_____

_____

_____

_____

Name: _____   Date: _____

_____

_____

_____

_____

_____

_____

_____

_____

_____

_____

_____

_____

_____

_____

_____

_____

Name: _____ Date: _____

_____

_____

_____

_____

_____

_____

_____

_____

_____

_____

_____

_____

_____

_____

_____

_____

_____

Name: _____   Date: _____

_____

_____

_____

_____

_____

_____

_____

_____

_____

_____

_____

_____

_____

_____

_____

_____

Name: _____   Date: _____

_____

_____

_____

_____

_____

_____

_____

_____

_____

_____

_____

_____

_____

_____

_____

_____

_____

_____

_____

_____

_____

_____

_____

_____

_____

_____

_____

_____

_____

_____

_____

_____

_____

_____

Name: _____   Date: _____

_____

_____

_____

_____

_____

_____

_____

_____

_____

_____

_____

_____

_____

_____

_____

_____

_____

Name: _____   Date: _____

_____

_____

_____

_____

_____

_____

_____

_____

_____

_____

_____

_____

_____

_____

_____

_____

Name: _____   Date: _____

_____

_____

_____

_____

_____

_____

_____

_____

_____

_____

_____

_____

_____

_____

_____

_____

_____

Name: _____   Date: _____

_____

_____

_____

_____

_____

_____

_____

_____

_____

_____

_____

_____

_____

_____

_____

_____

_____

Name: _____   Date: _____

_____

_____

_____

_____

_____

_____

_____

_____

_____

_____

_____

_____

_____

_____

_____

_____

_____

Name: _____   Date: _____

_____

_____

_____

_____

_____

_____

_____

_____

_____

_____

_____

_____

_____

_____

_____

_____

_____

Name: _____   Date: _____

_____

_____

_____

_____

_____

_____

_____

_____

_____

_____

_____

_____

_____

_____

_____

_____

_____

_____

Name: _____   Date: _____

_____

_____

_____

_____

_____

_____

_____

_____

_____

_____

_____

_____

_____

_____

_____

NOTES

NOTES

NOTES

NOTES